# Startups

# and

# Entrepreneurs

## Mistakes to Avoid For Success

ATTICUS ARISTOTLE

# CONTENTS

# Introduction

The Ford Edsel was a new line of cars introduced by Ford in 1957 that proved to be a major mistake costing the company 2.4 billion in today's dollars. Mistakes are made by novices and experts alike.

Successful entrepreneurs and investors alike will tell you the same thing: The product or idea itself is secondary. What matters most are the people behind the business. It isn't how smart the people are, how much experience they have, how much money they've saved and poured into the startup, or how many great ideas they came up with. What the investors care about most, and what makes the difference between failure and success, is the entrepreneur spirit. Do the people have the energy, drive, passion and hunger to make the business a success?

The idea itself is secondary. A great idea with the wrong people will fail, whereas a fair idea with the right person or people has a better chance of succeeding.

Investors who know how to spot a potentially successful startup aren't interested in an innovator or great thinker, unless that person is partnered with someone who has the entrepreneurial spirit. Someone who will always get funded is an innovator and thinker with the entrepreneurial spirit. That type of person will find a way to make almost every business a success.

The idea here is not to do what potential investors look for in order to get their support and money, simply because those things aren't constant, they are always changing. The purpose here is not to make the mistakes that cause new and successful businesses to fail, the mistakes that will cause investors and customers to walk away from your venture.

It is very difficult to teach someone all the things to do right in order to create a successful business. Many people get MBA's then spend the rest of their life trying to learn these things. Rather than trying to tell you all the right things, it is easier to tell you about the fixed number of reasons why businesses fail, the mistakes that will lead to the failure of your business if you aren't mindful of them.

If you're passionate about your startup, your drive will cause you to learn many of the things you need to become successful as you go along. Knowing the list of things that cause many businesses to fail will increase your chances for succeeding, giving you the benefit of experience from others, without having to endure it yourself.

Go through the list and prioritize those that apply to you at your current point in the startup. Review the list from time to time in order to re-prioritize the list. Avoiding the common mistakes will greatly improve your chances of creating a successful business. It is best to learn from other people's mistakes rather than to fail yourself and have others learn from your mistakes.

# How you treat your startup

## Treating your start-up as a hobby rather than a real company

Not realizing you have a real company really is a common way to fail. Treating the business as a project or hobby rather than a real company is a big mistake. The IRS treats something a person does for three years or more without making a profit as a hobby.

Unless you're happy with a new hobby, treat the startup as a real company, one with an actual impact if it fails, and acquire customers as quickly as possible.

This little test will help determine whether you're running your business as a hobby:

Is there a separate bank account in the name of the business or are you using your own personal account? A business would operate out of its own bank accounts, while a hobby would be managed from your own personal accounts. Even if you have no profits or income coming in, open that business account now.

Do you have a .gmail, .aol, .me, .yahoo or other type of mail account for your business? Any business related email accounts should use the businesses domain name, such as sales@mybusinessname.com.

Did you create an LLC, LLP or corporation for the business? If not, get that done immediately.

Are you using your home or personal cell phone as the main number for the business? This is extremely unprofessional and a turn off for many customers, unless of course, this is your hobby.

And the final test, profits. If you haven't generated any profits in three years or more, you probably should face the fact that you have an expensive hobby. It is time to move on and find another business that can generate profits. If you can afford to, and enjoy your hobby, then by all means, keep at it.

There are other things that make your business seem more like a hobby and may discourage customers. Look in the mirror and ask yourself, would you be a customer of this business? Think long and hard before answering, and if you can honestly answer 'yes', then you're on the right track.

## Acting like you're running a large corporation rather than a hungry startup

A successful corporate approach is not appropriate for small business startups. A startup is in a fight for survival. Acting as if you're part of a management committee making executive decisions doesn't work in a startup environment.

The management committee in a startup is everyone who works there, not a select group of entitled individuals. Don't try to run your startup as a small version of a large corporate enterprise. A startup requires a completely different management approach.

In addition to developing the business, startups need to develop world-class marketing, promotion, sales and support services. Normal corporate strategy, such as trying to increase sales by ten percent, doesn't work for a startup. To begin with, a startup needs to think in terms of increasing sales by hundreds of percentage points each year, quarter or even each month.

# Adapting

## Failure to adapt or change

It is said the only thing that is constant is change. Before investing money into an idea, ask yourself if it is still relevant. I created a website to capitalize on the 2012 end of the world craze. Unfortunately, by the time it was fully developed and ready for business, it was 2013. The venture naturally failed because I didn't bother to see if the concept was still relevant since the end of the world failed to materialize. Everyone moved on beyond 2012 but I neglected to change along with them, thinking there would be stragglers who were committed to the end of the world coming sooner rather than later, and so my product flopped.

Ideas and products evolve over time. Your finished product may look nothing like your original idea. Mold your idea to what your research and customers are telling you. Let the idea evolve over time. It's still your idea, but failure to listen to others who may have valuable input on changes that will make it a better product will result in a product no one wants.

Don't latch onto an idea, concept or business plan without

compromising and adapting until you run out of time and money.

Test your concept often, especially if your product launch gets delayed. Ask yourself, is the idea still relevant or has it become obsolete due to events or time? Marketing a product or service to address Y2K issues was a good business move in March of 1999, but not in Jan, 2000 or any time after that. Are you looking to sell cases for flip phones while most users have moved on to smart phones?

Learn to listen and to adapt to those you trust and especially to what the market, and your competition, is saying.

# Age

## Thinking you're too young or too old

It's not how old you are but how well you execute that matters most. Its sweat equity rather than age that really matters.

Don't let your age create a barrier for you. Don't blame your age if things don't go your way. If you weren't able to convince some potential investors to take a chance on your venture, it wasn't because of your age, but your pitch and presentation. Investors care about making money, regardless of whether it comes from a twelve or an eighty year old.

Opportunity, it seems, really doesn't discriminate. Regardless of age, sex, race, species or other consideration, all creatures are given the same exact chance.

Take for example Sean Belnick, who at fourteen saw an opportunity to sell furniture cheaper than anyone else: by eliminating the cost of a showroom and creating an online store. Belnick created his online store in 2001 from his bedroom with five hundred dollars which he used primarily to advertise his business. By the time Belnick was 22 years old his net value reached 42 million dollars.

Here are some more examples of young entrepreneurs executing and profiting from ideas most of us may have had in passing, but never took any further: https://quicken.intuit.com/support/help/fun-with-finances/9-young-entrepreneurs/INF16221.html

A 52 year old mixer salesman answered opportunities knock when he questioned why a restaurant was ordering more mixers than anyone else. The salesman recognized the owners had a unique model for selling food and persuaded them to expand nationally, opening restaurants across the country. Some people may not know who Ray Crock is, but everyone knows the restaurant chain he started: McDonald's.

# Assumptions

## Assuming if you build it they will come

If you don't know what happens when one assumes things, you may as well get out of the business of building a start-up. Never assume. Get hard facts, and revisit them often. Even hard facts become questionable due to changes in technology, the environment, the economy, demographics or even politics.

Assuming customers will come when you build it, instead of having a real marketing plan, will lead to a failure. If your product is going to fill a gap in the market, make sure customers are there waiting for something to come along.

Naturally, if you're creating something new, something customers don't know they want or need, then you must have a super marketing plan that tells them why they must have it. Customers with an unfulfilled need, hopefully the one you're working towards filling, have no problem signing on board early and waiting for the solution. Just don't keep them waiting too long from a promised date. If there really is a need for your service or product, getting customers ahead of time helps to confirm that you have a golden idea.

Another assumption is thinking profits are right around the corner since there's a need for the product. You need to figure out how much it will cost to acquire each customer, what your operating expense are and if customers are willing to pay the amount you need to charge to make a profit. If it's going to cost fifty dollars to acquire each customer and your profit per customer is only one dollar, you'll run out of money without any chance of making a profit. Buying something for a dollar and selling it for two will also drive you out of business because those kinds of returns aren't enough to cover customer acquisition and operating costs. The next section talks more about cash flow, profit margins and related mistakes.

Help in this area can be obtained by seasoned experts in one of the mentor programs, such as Score, or from websites such as Quora, where entrepreneurs congregate to get and offer help from each other.

# Luck

## Being in the wrong place at the wrong time

If you've ever played pool (billiards) or watched professionals play, you probably know about luck. Professional pool players appear to be lucky. Every shot they get is perfectly lined up. No matter how many balls they get into the pockets, the next shot is always an easy shot. They make their own luck. They can sink a ball and make the cue ball go exactly where they need to it go. This is why pool hustlers can make so much money. They know how to make you appear lucky, to play better than you normally play, so that you think you're better than they are. Naturally, your luck disappears when the bets become quite large. That's when all of the hustler's shots appear easy, while almost every one of yours looks impossible. Luck goes to the person who makes it happen.

There is always an element of luck that goes with starting up a new endeavor; however, in order to create that luck, you need to be in the right place at the right time. Running your startup from your home office might save you money, but you'll never be at the right location where a little bit of luck may strike, such as running into another entrepreneur who gives you a great tip.

There's a reason why many successful startups came out of certain areas such as Palo Alto, Seattle, Boston, New York and other hubs. If you can't be there in person, be there virtually: network and connect with others doing similar things.

Get yourself out there and known. Almost every person who happened to be at the right place at the right time worked extremely hard to make that happen. One thing is for certain: if you do nothing, luck will never find you. Get your name in the local newspaper, join your chamber of commerce and attend neighborhood events. Instead of hoping for the cue ball to go where you need it, give it a little push and perhaps luck will do the rest.

# Emotions

## Letting emotions get in the way of smart business decisions

In start-ups as in any corporate environment, there is no place for emotions. Those who tend to get emotional will not survive or get far in either environment.

Getting emotionally attached to an idea causes one to lose objectivity. Once that happens, everything is seen through rose colored glasses, thinking the idea is the best in the world and getting upset when others don't share the same point of view, instead of openly listening to constructive criticism.

When that happens, people begin to think they are always right and that others simply don't understand.

Putting your blood and guts into an endeavor is fully expected, but keep emotions out of it. When that happens, objectivity is lost and one fails to see clear signs when something is wrong, or accept constructive criticism that may result in a better product.

Stay clear headed and focused.

## Ego - Thinking you are the only one who can do it

Trying to do everything yourself will wear you out, cause you to lose focus and result in poor returns on your sweat equity. Don't be afraid to share the work with others. Hire competent staff to share the workload, and empower them to make decisions in their field of expertise.

Empowering others who share your vision is required in order to succeed and convince others to back you.

Don't let your ego get in the way of sharing the workload and asking for help or advice when you need it. Learning as you go along instead of thinking you know everything will improve the chances for your venture to succeed. One word of caution: watch who you ask for advice. There will be some who will give you the wrong or conflicting advice to keep you from succeeding, either due to jealousy, hatred or competition.

One way to determine if your ego is getting the better of you is to see how much work you delegate to others, if any. If you're doing everything yourself and not delegating anything, then your ego is getting the upper hand.

Always remember: you're really not as good at everything as you think you are. Delegating motivates others, and usually gets more work done than if you try to do everything yourself.

## Constantly afraid others will steal your idea: Thinking it's just as classified as the recipe to coke.

Take off the top secret classification; there is no need for it: no one is going to steal your idea, that is, until you've proven it works. Failing to share your idea because you don't want others to steal it is a very common mistake.

It's not the idea that really matters, but how it is executed. In all likelihood, thousands of others had the same idea, and some may have even tried to execute on that idea. The one who will come out on top is the person who executes it the best. Exerting extra effort to keep the idea a secret will end up costing you in the long run.

People and companies who are able to execute on an idea already have many ideas already lined up. They'll wait to see how well you can execute your idea, and then offer to buy it from you instead of trying to execute it themselves. Google and most other successful startups know it's about execution. They aren't interested in hearing new ideas, they want to see them executed successfully, and will then pursue the startup, not the idea. Building an idea from the ground up takes time and hard work. Nobody wants to go through all of that when someone's already done it. It's much safer for the larger companies to make a reasonable offer for the startup if they really want the idea.

What usually becomes valuable in the long run is the team you've put together to execute the idea. The idea itself becomes secondary. Do an outstanding job of executing an idea and investors will back your next startup, regardless of which idea is being pursued.

Those afraid others are going to steal their idea tend to keep things to themselves, resulting in missed opportunities and chances to get great feedback that may improve the idea.

Some will be afraid others will think they are being silly so they hide what they're doing, waiting for it to be successful before telling anyone. If it's so silly that they have to hide what they're doing, chances are it will fail since they aren't investing as much time as they should and aren't getting any feedback or support from those around.

Some are afraid investors will take their idea and run with it themselves, resulting in potential investors walking away the business, regardless of how much potential it has. Investors are tired of people with great ideas or those who feel they can't trust anyone. They want to see people who can execute, regardless of what the idea is. Prove you have the drive, determination and skill and have already implemented the idea and proven that it works. That's what investors want to see.

Chances are many others before you already came up with the idea but never executed. Some may have executed but not effectively. Everyone will know what the idea is once it goes public, so keeping it secret hurts you more than it helps. Execute the idea better than anyone else and it won't matter who tries to copy or steal it.

# Focus

## Focusing on multiple ideas rather than one main idea

Many entrepreneurs are constantly coming up with new ideas that seem even better than the one before. Spending time on these will cause you to spread yourself and your resources thin, or miss the right opportunity. Focus on the idea that has the best timing and potential and leave the others alone until you're ready to move on to the next idea. One at a time will allow you to focus 100% on executing that idea, increasing the chances for succeeding.

Once you've set your goals and objectives, stick to them. Learn to focus on the here and now. There will be plenty of opportunities for the other ideas once the current one becomes a success.

## Looking for investors too soon

Looking for investors takes the focus away from where it should be: running the business. Investors are more interested in the person running the startup and signs of market acceptance before even considering investing in a startup. If you don't have a reputation for creating a successful venture, and don't have any income coming in, investors will not be interested.

Rather than spending all of your time working on the investor pitch, work on acquiring customers and users instead. Spend too much time looking for investors and you'll end up getting frustrated to the point where you'll give up. Focus instead on where you have the most control, can do the most good, and can see positive results: delivering the product or service your customers are waiting for.

# Cash flow – Budgeting and Profit Margins

## Not properly managing your cash flow

In other words, running out of money

Not only do you need enough operating cash to sustain the business for at least three months, you also need to have enough liquid cash on hand to use for emergencies and special occasions.

Many entrepreneurs forget that cash is being spent every single day, through salaries, rent, utilities, and other expenses so unless cash is coming in that's greater than the cash going out, the business will run out of money fairly quickly.

Be careful where and how much money is spent. Create a budget so you'll know exactly where it will go and how long it will last. Until cash starts flowing in, watch where the money goes and save every receipt, no matter how small.

During the start-up stage, cash will be your most important asset, guard it very carefully.

Too much cash can be equally dangerous. Only borrow or get from investors only what you really need. Having too much cash on hand creates a false sense of security, causing one to spend more than necessary.

If you're not good at managing money, get someone on board who's an excellent financial planner, and don't be afraid to ask for advice from those who are good at it. Look at it this way: if your personal finances are a mess and you have no idea how to balance a checkbook, get someone who is to manage the business finances.

## Thinking that a 100% profit margin is good enough

If you fail to realize that real margins are have to be much more than buy for one and sell for 2. A one hundred percent margin won't keep you in business. You margins need to be more like buy for one and sell for ten.

Many startups don't realize that margins need to take into account all of the costs required to fund a sustainable business. This includes all salaries, marketing, promotion, rental, utilities and every other thing the business has to spend money on. The cost for all of those expenses needs to be covered in the cost of your product, at a price in line or better than your competition, or one that your customers are willing to pay.

Things that go into the cost of your product may include:

1. Materials used to build the product
2. Factory charges
3. Packaging and Distribution
4. Office expenses (supplies, high speed access, phones and utilities)
5. Salaries, wages, employee benefits and payroll taxes
6. Marketing, promotions and other sales expenditures
7. Insurance
8. Real estate costs (rent, taxes, insurance, repairs)
9. Consulting fees
10. Other miscellaneous expenses

All of these expenses need to be considered when pricing your product. A high price can be justified if the product is superior to the competition and customers are willing to pay the premium. A lower price than the competition can be achieved if these costs can be kept below what others are spending.

## Not understanding that it takes one and a half to three years to reach breakeven point

It can take anywhere from one and a half to three years to reach the breakeven point for your startup. That's not making a profit, but to recover exactly how much you're spending each month. This means you need to have enough capital on hand to support the business during that time period.

There are many websites that can help you determine your breakeven point by taking in your expenses, expected revenue per unit, cost per unit. These apps can tell you how many units need to be sold and how much cash has to be taken in per month to break even. Anything above that would be considered profit.

If you need to generate $20,000 in sales each month and only generate $8,000, there needs to be enough cash on hand to cover that $12,000 shortfall. If this happens for ten months, $120,000 will be needed on hand to support the business.

Knowing this information up front can save those without enough cash on hand lots of time and money. Unless there is a deep pocketed partner, it is best to keep operating costs down to a minimum until the breakeven point is reached and profits can be generated.

## Scrimping where it really counts

Buying your clothing from the clearance rack might be fine when resources are tight, but it's not alright when it comes to a product you want others to spend their money or their time on. Scrimping, or going bargain basement, on the product will hurt you in the long run. Spend what's needed in order to deliver a quality product. If you don't have the resources to create a quality product, borrow or wait until you do. Buy everything you personally need from the clearance racks in order to save enough to create a quality product.

Your potential customers will know if you've cut corners and won't buy from you or use your website. Leave the graphics work to an expert. Knowing your way around Photoshop doesn't make you a design expert. Customers can tell the difference between a professional job and one that's done by an amateur.

Go cheap on your coffee, donuts and other non critical expenses, although for some, those are critical expenditures, but don't go cheap when it comes to your customers. There are companies that will build a website for three thousand dollars and others that will do it for twenty thousand. There are companies that will market your product for one thousand while others will demand twenty five thousand.

You get what you paid for, and scrimping where it really counts can cause your startup to fail. Not only that, you'll wonder why it failed for you and worked for the next team that developed that idea. It's because they didn't scrimp where it counted.

# People - (Founders, CEO's, Partners and Staff)

## Thinking that as a founder you're equally qualified to be a CEO

The skills required for a CEO are much different than those for a founder. Simply because you've founded one or more successful companies doesn't automatically make you qualified to be a CEO, especially as the business grows.

The skills for a founder, passionate, visionary and able to fully execute do not translate into those required for a CEO: ability to implement policy, human resource skills and partnerships.

There are some entrepreneurs who can do both, but most can't. Understanding and accepting your limitations is very difficult, especially when it appears like you're taking a back seat, however, for the company to succeed, it's something that must be done.

## Picking the wrong co-founders or partners

The success or failure of the business will depend greatly on the strengths and weaknesses of the founders and partners. Picking too many or the wrong ones can derail your chances of success.

Picking the right partner is a huge responsibility and one of the first major decisions made when starting a business. Make sure you pick someone you can work with, is trustworthy, fully committed, and compliments your skills.

Getting partners who aren't as committed to the success of the startup as you are will kill moral and ruin the business. Everyone needs to put in 110% effort and the same amount of time. Partners who are never there or only involved part time will hurt you.

Having a partner with the wrong skills is just as bad. A partner that complements your skills, or has deep pockets is what's required

Here are some of the things to avoid in a partner:

1.  Uncommitted: Unable to commit an equal amount of time and money, or more money to make up for time constraints or additional time to make up for money constraints.

2.  Risk averse: Someone who needs regular work hours and a steady income.

3.  Over Analyzer: This is the perfectionist who does into analysis paralysis each time something needs to be done. This type is all talk but very little action.

4. Excuses: Always has an excuse why something couldn't be done. Usually has problems at home or other personal issues, causing the startup to take a back seat.

5. The Friend: Has the right skills but can't leave a good paying job just at this moment. Will lend a hand when able to until the company generates millions, as which point can leave well-paying job in favor of equity in this startup that can be sold right away. Special projects at work will always come up just when those skills are most needed.

6. Idea person: The person with the idea. Ideas are worthless without the right execution. Partnering with someone with a good idea and nothing else to bring to the table is a bad idea. This usually means you're taking all of the risk in return for half of the profit.

7. The expert: Has written dozens of books on the matter but has never been involved with a startup. Will end up spending all your money on the lecture circuit, which conveniently help sell his books, which you have no stake in.

8. The Yes man: Agrees with everything you say. Never argues or presents own opinion. Agrees with you even when making a drastic mistake.

9. Mr. Right: Is never wrong and argues with you over every single decision. Loves to hear himself speak and fills the entire meeting with his take on everything, preventing the actual agenda from being discussed.

There are many other things to look out for in a partner, so be extremely careful how and who you choose.

## Hiring managers instead of leaders

Many CEO's hire senior executives from large established organizations; wrongly thinking they will be just as effective in a startup. Many of these executives are managers who are good at, and accustomed to, leading through a bureaucratic hierarchy. That type of manager will kill moral and vision in a startup environment, essentially killing any chances for success.

When looking to hire senior level staff, hire those who are true leaders rather than managers. Same with new graduates, don't hire the ones with the highest grades, but go after the ones who were always exploring and venturing off, the ones who look up to visionaries rather than executives.

A leader inspires others while a manager simply gets the work done. Leading visionaries is not a skill one acquires through schooling. Look for a leader who inspires vision and creativity rather than a process oriented manager.

Also, keep clear of hiring friends and relatives because you feel obligated or like hanging out with them. Hire them only if they have the skill set needed for the job and both of you can be completely unbiased towards each other.

Lastly, steer clear of hiring your doubles, those with the same qualities, experience and talents that you possess. Do you really want your double working alongside of you? You'll clash like there's no tomorrow! What are needed are those who compliment you, to fill in the gaps.

## Hiring too late and issuing equity too early

The time to hire is just before you need it. Waiting until the demand requires it, when orders start going out later than expected and customers have to wait longer before reaching someone, is too late.

The way to prevent this is by measuring productivity. How productive is your business and how much can it manage with current resources? Each week, see how the productivity trend is going. Identify a point on your productivity trending reports when you will not be able to meet demand with current resources. Estimate how long it will take to reach that point, then begin hiring several months before that point is reached. If you wait until reaching or exceeding capacity before hiring, customer service will be impacted, causing you to lose customers and leaving you with too many hands on deck.

Some people you hire early on may only have a half-hearted commitment and ambitions of their own.

When first starting out you want to attract people who are excited about and committed to the business, and want to be involved because they believe in you and the idea. People with that kind of enthusiasm will do what it takes to help make the business a success.

Wait a reasonable time period, and until you're convinced they are committed to the business, before offering equity or stock options.

The problem with giving these out too soon is the staff member may walk out on you, leaving you to work twice as hard to make the business a success, while they enjoy the benefits of your labor.

# Skills

## Not learning every aspect of your business

As an entrepreneur, you need to be skilled in every aspect of your business. You don't have to be a specialist in every field, but know enough to be able to perform any task as needed. This means in addition to being a visionary, you need to know tech support, sales, marketing, the product and any other field associated with your business.

The purpose of knowing every aspect isn't for the entrepreneur to perform them all, but to understand what needs to be done, how it should be done and to provide guidance, assistance and well informed decisions when called for.

Knowledge is king and knowing every aspect of the business increases the entrepreneur's chances for succeeding. It also makes it difficult for others to get over by sounding knowledgeable and professional, while they don't really know anything.

This becomes less important as the startup gets larger, but when first starting out, not being familiar with every aspect of the business will become an obstacle.

If you've ever watched the television show Shark Tank, you've seen what the investors do to someone not familiar with every aspect of their business. Those investors are there to make money and know that a venture has a much better of succeeding if the entrepreneur knows every aspect of the business.

Not everyone needs to know everything if there are multiple founders: the combined skill set should cover the skills requirement.

# Communication

## Not having or communicating clear goals and vision

Every business, no matter how big or small needs goals. Failing to set a clear set of achievable goals will result in delays in achieving profitability, threatening your cash flow.

Knowing exactly what you want your business to achieve is like a pilot with a flight plan. It helps guide you, let's you know you're on the right path and gives you a target, with a timeline.

Setting long and short term goals allows one to plan effectively and measure progress along the way.

Your vision is your ultimate long term goal. Document your goals and vision and make sure everyone working for you understands and strives for both. Having a vision and letting your staff know where they're headed helps motivate them, increasing your chances for succeeding.

## Not getting everyone working on the same thing

Valuable time and resources are lost when everyone is focusing on something different. Thinking the development team is hard at work on your website when it turns out they've been coding a feature it was decided not to implement can lead to unnecessary delays.

Even small teams working in the same building can get out of sync. Without regular meetings where everyone discusses what they're working on and any issues which may have come up, valuable time will be lost.

Keep the team involved with what's going on and any changes that have been made. Making changes without informing everyone, thinking they will object, is poor leadership. Everyone should be on board if the change is worth making, and any who aren't should be listened to. They may have a valid point to make which may cause you to revisit the reason for the change or to make further adjustments which may improve the change even more.

Just because no one says anything doesn't mean they all agree with you or that they understand what's in your head. Solicit feedback from your partners and staff to make sure they know and agree with what's in your head. Better yet, create an open environment where every team member is allowed to speak their mind, not just when asked, or only to those at a certain level. One of them may have a great suggestion that would turn a good idea into a killer idea. Someone may also have a solution to a problem you or one of your technical experts has that would speed up time to market.

Open lines of communication can make the difference, not just within the team, but with your investors and customers. Keep everyone up to date on your product's status. Delivering something that isn't what your customers or investors envisioned will kill your startup and your credibility.

It is even more critical to communicate to everyone when you hit a bump in the road and miss a *target deadline*, even for a small milestone. Everyone understands this happens from time to time. This may not seem like it matters much, but when you overcome that bump, there will be that much more excitement for your startup and your abilities to overcome obstacles. It may also get you help from areas you never expected: others may have hit the same bump and found a solution that they're willing to share. Sharing your progress, including stumbles and wins, shows you care enough to involve customers. They'll show their appreciation by helping you solve those bumps, and more importantly, sharing your wins with others.

# Competition

## Ignoring or wasting too much time on what the competition is doing

Spending too much time watching and copying the competition will result in a product exactly like theirs, instead of something better. You'll be known as a copycat rather than an innovator and will not reach your targets. While you need to be aware of what your competition is doing, spending too much time watching them will detract you from where you're needed the most.

Ignoring the competition is equally, if not more, important. One of the things in regards to competition is trying to understand why they are successful. Try to learn what they're doing right and what they're doing wrong. Capitalize on their mistakes while trying to adopt things they are doing that are attracting and retaining customers.

No matter what, if your competition begins increasing market share, find out why in order to determine if you need to make any changes to your strategy.

Research in Motion (RIM), the maker of the Blackberry device, had close to a 100% share of the corporate and government market. When the Smartphone came along, RIM ignored the competition. It continued to do so until it went bankrupt. While corporate buyers remained loyal to RIM, corporate workers who used the devices stopped doing so, forcing companies to find solutions for supporting Smart phones.

Your competition may not always go after your market share in the manner you would expect. Learn to look for the unexpected: Are they going after your end user, which is what Apple and Samsung did, after your supplier (remember the steel shortage?) or after your distribution channel. Apple, Samsung and book publishers ignored Amazon when it came out with a very inexpensive book reader, the Kindle. That device allowed Amazon to corner the eBook market, which in turn allowed it to control pricing, competition and publisher profit margins.

Many retailers have low price guarantees, where they'll match a competitor's price. Wal-Mart takes this one step further. Rather than requiring you to bring an ad with the competition's lower price, Wal-Mart advertises they do it for you, automatically adjusting prices each week to match competitor sale prices. This tells customers and everyone else that Wal-Mart is aware of what the competition is doing, and adjusting to meet the challenge. It also allows Wal-Mart to ignore a price cut if it's too steep, without customers being aware that an item was missed.

# Customers

## Not acquiring and retaining customers

Regardless of how great your idea is and how many people love it; if customers aren't acquired you'll be out of business before you know it.

Once you acquire customers, you need to retain them; otherwise you'll be spending more to acquire customers than what you make from them.

Do whatever it takes to acquire and retain customers. Word of mouth can either make or break a business. Ignore or treat your customers badly and you'll lose much more than a few customers: you'll love everyone they interact with on social media, and everyone those people interacts with.

When going after customers, make sure you go after the right ones. One of the questions frequently asked by venture capital investors is 'how much does it cost you to acquire a costumer?" Going after women of all ages when your product is made to help pregnant women will substantially increase your customer acquisition costs, and reduce profits. The same with pricing: go after high income earners rather than everyone if you will be offering a high priced luxury item. While it's nice to feel everyone will want to buy your product or service, there will always be a specific target to market to. Acquire those customers first and others will follow along through word of mouth.

Naturally, once you acquire those customers, your acquisition costs can be kept low by retaining them: this is easily done by giving them what they want, at the time, price and condition promised. After that, all you have to do is be available to answer any questions they have. It's quite simple, indeed. I really don't understand why the wireless cell phone carriers have a hard time doing that. Wireless companies have such a high customer acquisition rate, mainly because they have a hard time delivering what they promise, that they will actually try to pay customers not to leave. Try to cancel your cell phone service by phone and the customer service agent your speaking to will transfer you to the retention department, which will offer you incentives, including money, to stay.

# Features and Feedback

## Overcomplicating your product or business

Don't add too many features. It's much more difficult to make something easy and intuitive than to create something with tons of bells and whistles. Apple grew into a powerhouse by living by the principle of keeping things simple. Anyone can make something complicated that does everything you could ever need, but it takes a real genius to create something simple enough that you can actually use.

The majority of your target wants something that does everything, but doesn't want to devote the time to learn how to use it. Make it complex internally, but simple and intuitive externally for the customer.

## Trying to create a product for everyone

You'll fail if you try to create a product for everyone. If you try to please everyone you'll end up pleasing no one. Pick a target audience and make the product work for that target.

The business or product can expand later, after establishing a base. The right business or product is simple, compelling, and aligned with the business goals and a specific target customer base.

One of the first points that should be clearly developed is a specific customer base to target. With that in mind, design the business or product to deliver value to those specific customers, not something that would appeal to everyone. Others may see value and perhaps buy your product, but if you try to target everyone up front, very few will end up buying your product.

## Not seeking feedback or ignoring what your customers are saying

Ignore your customers and you'll do so at your own peril. Customers can tell you what's wrong with your product and help you deliver something others will love to use. They may not tell you what to build or how to build it, but they can tell you if it's broken, what doesn't work, or exactly what they like or dislike about it.

Pre-filtering feedback to support your idea is just as bad as not seeking feedback. Listen to feedback with an open mind, instead of picking only the feedback which supports your way of thinking or positive feedback. Ignoring negative or constructive feedback will result in a reduction in repeat business and an increase in marketing expenses.

Feedback from friends, relatives, investors, VC's and other entrepreneurs is not the same as feedback from actual customers. Customer feedback tends to be unbiased and more in tune with your market.

# Low hanging fruit

## Going for the big picture rather than the easy stuff

Nothing kills moral and turns off potential investors and customers than seeing no progress over a long period of time. (Real business vs. hobby)

While it would be great to come out of the gate with everything as planned and ahead of schedule, things don't always work out that way.

In order to keep others interested in your startup, show you are making progress, no matter how small it is. (Communication)

Separate your goals into smaller easy to reach milestones. Look for any low hanging fruit, and milestones, deliverables, project steps that are easy and quick to complete. Take care of those first. This gets the easy stuff out of the way, helping you and your team members remain focused on the big stuff. It also shows progress that you can advertise to your potential customers and investors. Progress is progress, no matter how small it is.

As you complete each milestone, no matter how small, update your project status and presentation material. Going after low hanging fruit increases team moral by showing progress, regardless of how small it is. (Communication/Teamwork)

For example, instead of setting a goal to complete an entire application, break it up into smaller goals, such as the individual sub-functions within the application. Look for the simple sub-functions and complete those first. Even if each sub-function is one percent of the project, showing increases from 1%, 2%, to 3% over a three week period is much better than showing 0% week after week.

Be clear on what's been accomplished, how much remains, where you are headed, and any help you may need with the remaining work. You'll be pleasantly surprised at how much other people can help you, with things like knowledge, money, connections and other ways you never anticipated.

Going after and completing low hanging fruit supercharges your team, your customers and your investors. It shows you can meet target dates, no matter how small, and will make missing the big date that much less stressful.

# Market share - Promotion and Marketing

## Waiting until the idea is fully developed before promoting it

Begin promoting and selling the product before it's built. Many companies promote a new product long before its ready, and most begin taking preorders shortly before the product is ready for sales.

Movie studios begin advertising a movie months before its scheduled release date. The same goes with book publishers. Marketing the product long before its release date creates a buzz that keeps growing.

Don't wait until your product launches to start promoting it. Begin promotion long before its ready, doing almost everything one would do when the product is launched. Go on several blog tours to talk about the product and the development status. Get early reviewers to give their opinion of the upcoming product.

By the time the startup goes live, there should already be a pretty good market share of customers just waiting for that starting bell. This gets the business out of the starting gate with a clamoring of anxious customers, generating even more buzz and attracting others and possibly the media.

Implement your marketing plan about three months before launch date. If you don't have one, then this is the time to develop it, and in a hurry. Build your plan while marking the upcoming launch. This will give you an opportunity to see what works and what doesn't. You can even begin making pre-shipment sales, in much the same way that DVD movies, books, phones and other products are sold before they actually begin shipping. When going the pre-sales route, there needs to be a firm shipping date. It is fine for Apple to miss a shipping date, but not for a startup.

## Not understanding that brilliant marketing and distribution is what sells

Over and over again there is a product that goes viral, with everyone asking why? It's not such a great product. It's not something anyone needs. It's not even unique or innovative. But yet it's generating millions in sales.

One advertising executive who understood this is well known for making the biggest success of selling a totally useless object. In 1975, Gary Dahl convinced 1.5 million people they needed to own a pet rock, at $3.95 each. More recently, an app which does one thing, lets you send an audible 'Yo' to another app user, was downloaded by 50,000 users in just three months, allowing the creator to raise 1 million dollars from investors.

Another example is the hula hoop. Most people don't know the original hula hoop had been around for centuries as an exercise device. It had usually been made out of wood or other hard substance and wasn't very popular. In 1957, Richard Knerr and Arthur Melin, saw the Australian bamboo "exercise hoops" and created their own version out of light weight, brightly colored, plastic. Their marketing campaign was so successful they sold twenty five million plastic hula hoops in the first four months, and over 200 million within two years.

An average product with brilliant packaging, marketing and distribution is more likely to succeed than a great product with poor marketing and distribution.

There have been many products which seemed to be failures until someone came along with a better marketing strategy. Many will tell you, a so-so product with good marketing trumps a better product almost every time.

Don't build a better product just to have someone steal your thunder by doing a better job of marketing a weak imitation. Build a great product, and then implement a brilliant marketing plan to let everyone know it.

Then make sure they can get it when you tell them they will. Keep them waiting and they'll go elsewhere.

If the orders start coming in and you're unable to deliver or can't keep up with a modest demand, then your customers will begin to disappear. A brilliant marketing job will only work if your entire distribution channel is ready. Unexpected demand is one thing and completely understandable, but not being ready to ship or to support expected sales projections can be disastrous.

Make sure the entire distribution chain, everything required to move the product from the factory to the end user, is ready. If it's a new distribution network, test it to make sure everything works as expected, long before you're ready to launch. If you don't have a distribution channel ready, look at what your competition is using and consider doing the same thing, at least until you're off the ground.

## Promoting features rather than benefits

People don't buy something because it has great features; they buy something for what it can do for them.

If promoting a website, rather than saying it was written using the best programming language; tell them it will save them time by reducing keystrokes and giving instant responses. Rather than say 'using state of the art encryption', tell them it will protect their data.

If you are going to list the features, then include the advantages they provide, and the benefits to the customer for each feature.

1. Each car comes with the best steel belted radial tires.

2. Each car comes with the best steel belted radial tires, allowing the car to hug the road in any situation.

3. Each car comes with the best steel belted radial tires, allowing the car to hug the road in any situation, because your safety requires it.

Not everyone will know the benefits of having steel belted radial tires. Not everyone will think they need a car that hugs the road; they'll think it's something only useful for speeders. When you tell them it's for their safety, more will understand and feel better knowing they are included.

Customers buy things that are beneficial to them and are blind to the outstanding and competitor-beating features that your creative minds came up with. Tell them what those outstanding features will do for them.

One important thing to keep in mind: All of your customers may not have the same needs, and their needs may change from time to time, or due to circumstance. For example, someone with money may not be as concerned with how much money can be saved by using your product. They might be more interested in saving time rather than money. A mother with a large household or who entertains often might be more interested in an oven that can cook more items simultaneously over one with a warming feature.

Target features to the right people, at the right time.

# Practice what you preach

## Not using your own product

If you're selling a product and feel it isn't for you, why would you think it's great for everyone else?

If you develop a killer website and find yourself not using it, why should anyone else use it?

Use your product, your app and your website. Learn every nuance about each. Understand every aspect so when someone points something out to you, you'll know exactly what they're talking about, and convincing them that you're worth dealing with. If others find that you don't use your own products and aren't very knowledgeable on how they work, why should they waste their time? If they feel you're too busy for your own product, they will be too busy as well.

Using your product also helps you identify problems that may kill sales, or give you ideas for improving it.

Don't lie about it either, others will see right through your lies.

When Steve Jobs gave a presentation about the Apples latest gadget, he knew every nuance of the product. Jobs didn't have to read from a teleprompter or look at a presentation in order to talk about the features. He knew them instinctively. How many times have you seen someone give a pitch about a product they weren't very familiar with? That company lost a potential customer each time the presenter hit a glitch during the demo.

# Worrying about capacity

## Devoting time to users who aren't there

Worry about getting the product out and in use by customers before worrying about being able to support millions of customers. Don't waste valuable resources ordering and configuring fifty servers when five are more than enough to handle expected demand. It's simple, fast and inexpensive to add capacity as demand increases. It is much better to add five more servers a month later to meet demand than to delay product launch waiting for fifty servers to be configured and tested.

It's one thing to worry about hundreds of thousands of customers on day one, but don't spend time, money and other resources to prepare for it, then to wind up with only a few hundred. Worry more about getting the product ready, available and everything in place to support a realistic amount of traffic.

Validate your actual demand and resource requirements with real customers first. Worry about adding extra capacity when the time comes. If you spend too much time worrying, it may never happen.

Additional capacity is easy to add if demand requires it. Lost time, money and resources spent to create a massive website or distribution channel for demand that doesn't materialize can never be recovered. The times when companies such as Facebook, Twitter and others faced unprecedented demand happen very rarely and usually for special events, where demand is known but not properly accounted for, or exceeds expectations. In either case, the problem is quickly solved by adding additional capacity to meet demand.

# When to give up

## Quitting too soon

Quitting is not the same as giving up on a failing product. Don't let circumstances force you into giving up on something that you know will succeed. Do whatever you need to do in order to turn those circumstances around.

Many opportunities were lost because someone gave up too early. Before WhatsApp came about, there were many web based messaging services that allowed users to text from the web, bypassing carrier texting fees. If those companies hung around a bit longer to catch the Smartphone revolution, they could have had the deal that ultimately went to the founders of WhatsApp. I happen to know this because they would have been the competition I was hoping to beat out with my own messaging platform.

My messaging platform would have done the same thing that WhatsApp does, except much sooner. My partners and I even had a waiting list of customers, but we failed to execute properly, committing some of the mistakes mentioned in this book: our product was never completed, first because we worked with friends who offered to develop the app in their spare time. It stalled a second time when our developer took off, taking code that was 95% completed. After that I simply quit, even though I knew we had a winning product.

If you know you have a winning idea, especially when you have customers waiting for it, don't quit, no matter which obstacles may cross your path.

## Holding onto a failing product

Don't hold onto a product when there are signs it won't generate any return, or the returns needed to justify the amount of resources put into it. Allowing the product to fail allows you to save valuable resources that can be utilized for the next product or idea.

Aside from sustained losses, there are other signs that may tell you it's time to let go. These signs include:

You no longer recommend your product or service to people you know.

You're main concern is getting investors back their money.

It doesn't feel right hiring, or keeping, the best workers or people you know.

You think those working with you deserve better.

You no longer care what customers are saying.

# Summary

Starting a business venture is extremely difficult and requires dedication, hard work and focus. There are many ways to create a successful business, by following conventional methods or new untested areas: Michael Dell became a billionaire by building computer upgrade kits in his college dorm room. Dell recognized an opportunity for selling computers directly from the warehouse, bypassing the middleman (local computer stores) to consumers and businesses, at the time a new business model in the high priced computer industry.

What remains constant, for startups and entrepreneurs alike, are the ways new startups can fail. About 90% of startups fail, which means that only one in ten will succeed. There are many reasons why ten percent succeed, however, the ninety percent that failed made one or a combination of the mistakes listed in this book.

See which topics apply to your startup and find ways to avoid making the same mistakes. Trying to remember hundreds of things that successful businesses did to succeed is a difficult feat, but learning the mistakes to avoid is something manageable.

When you reach the point where you have a viable business, you can then try to get funding for growth. However, there are some things to consider before approaching investors.

Investors are usually interested in one thing: making money. They want the greatest return they can get on their investment. Between two startups, one that can return a 100% return on investment and one that can return 5000%, an investor will fund the one second one. A 100% return on an investment may not be worth all of the risk involved. A 100% return for you might be acceptable, but for investors who are constantly risking time and money, they need the highest possible return, to cover losses they may have suffered from other startups.

Some of the things investors look for include:

You've properly valued the startup – investors won't even bother to look at a very promising business if the valuation is way off.

Repeatability – you or your team have successfully launched a startup and are now working on the second, third or fourth.

Have a product with a proven need.

Your target customers are in a large and growing market.

You and your partners have real expertise in the market. Don't create a new soda drink if you have absolutely no experience in the beverage industry.

Business can grow and expand – it is a repeatable business model.

Selling homemade strawberry preserves is not a scalable business – there is a limit to the number of jars you can make.

You have something that makes you better than the competition. What makes your product or service better than the competition? Is yours better made at a lower cost? Do you have a better distribution channel? Is there room in market for you and your product? You need something that distinguishes you from the competition so they can't turn around and steal your customers out from under you.

If you're creating an app, program or website, what makes you better than the others, and is it able to easily integrate with other? Does it use new technology? Have you partnered with companies like Google, Dell, HP or other known entity?

Do you have industry support? Do you have an established fan base?

Are you a leader with integrity, passion, totally committed, decisive, flexible, calm and collected under pressure, and willing to take constructive criticism and advice? There were many times on Shark Tank where the investors loved the idea and wanted to invest but wouldn't do so because of the stubbornness of the founder.

# Other Titles

Mark Cuban's essential entrepreneurial tools:

"Cold Calling Techniques" by Stephan Schiffman

*This easy-to-follow guide helps you beat today's cold calling obstacles, such as voice mail, cell phones, and e-mail.*

"Rework" by Jason Fried

*Most business books give you the same old advice: Write a business plan, study the competition, seek investors, yadda yadda. If you're looking for a book like that, put this one back on the shelf.*

*Rework shows you a better, faster, easier way to succeed in business. Read it and you'll know why plans are actually harmful, why you don't need outside investors, and why you're better off ignoring the competition. The truth is, you need less than you think. You don't need to be a workaholic.*

*You don't need to staff up. You don't need to waste time on paperwork or meetings. You don't even need an office. Those are all just excuses.*

## Hackers & Painters: Big Ideas of the Computer Age by Paul Graham

*Consider these facts: Everything around us is turning into computers. Your typewriter is gone, replaced by a computer. Your phone has turned into a computer. So has your camera. Soon your TV will. Your car was not only designed on computers, but has more processing power in it than a room-sized mainframe did in 1970. Letters, encyclopedias, newspapers, and even your local store are being replaced by the Internet.*

*Hackers & Painters: Big Ideas from the Computer Age, by Paul Graham, explains this world and the motivations of the people who occupy it. In clear, thoughtful prose that draws on illuminating historical examples, Graham takes readers on an unflinching exploration into what he calls "an intellectual Wild West."*

*The ideas discussed in this book will have a powerful and lasting impact on how we think, how we work, how we develop technology, and how we live. Topics include the importance of beauty in software design, how to make wealth, heresy and free speech, the programming language renaissance, the open-source movement, digital design, internet startups, and more.*

## The Innovator's Dilemma by Clayton Christensen

*The Innovator's Dilemma presents a set of rules for capitalizing on the phenomenon of disruptive innovation.*
*Find out:*
*When it is right not to listen to customers.*

*When to invest in developing lower-performance products that promise lower margins.*
*When to pursue small markets at the expense of seemingly larger and more lucrative ones.*

Art of the Start by Guy Kawasaki

*A new product, a new service, a new company, a new division, a new organization, a new anything — where there's a will, here's the way.*

*It begins with a dream that just won't quit, the once-in-a-lifetime thunderbolt of pure inspiration, the obsession, the world-beater, the killer app, the next big thing. Everyone who wants to make the world a better place becomes possessed by a grand idea.*

*But what does it take to turn your idea into action?*

*Whether you are an entrepreneur, intrapreneur, or not-for-profit crusader, there's no shortage of advice available on issues such as writing a business plan, recruiting, raising capital, and branding. In fact, there are so many books, articles, and Web sites that many startups get bogged down to the point of paralysis. Or else they focus on the wrong priorities and go broke before they discover their mistakes.*

*In The Art of the Start, Guy Kawasaki brings two decades of experience as one of business's most original and irreverent strategists to offer the essential guide for anyone starting anything, from a multinational corporation to a church group. At Apple in the 1980s, he helped lead one of the great companies of the century, turning ordinary consumers into evangelists. As founder and CEO of Garage Technology Ventures, a venture capital firm, he has field-tested his ideas with dozens of newly hatched companies. And as the author of bestselling business books and articles, he has advised thousands of people who are making their startup dreams real.*

*From raising money to hiring the right people, from defining your positioning to creating a brand, from creating buzz to buzzing the competition, from managing a board to fostering a community, this book will guide you through an adventure that's more art than science — the art of the start.*

## Word of Mouth Marketing by Andy Sernovitz

*Master the art of word of mouth marketing with this practical hands-on guide.*

*With straightforward advice and humor, marketing expert Andy Sernovitz will show you how the world's most respected and profitable companies get their best customers for free through the power of word of mouth.*

*Learn the five essential steps that make word of mouth work and everything you need to get started using them. Understand the real purpose of blogs, communities, viral email, evangelists, and buzz--when to use them and how simple it is to make them work.*

*Learn what sparks the irrepressible enthusiasm of Apple and TiVo fans. Understand why everyone is talking about a certain restaurant, car, band, or dry cleaner--and why other businesses and products are ignored. Discover why some products become huge successes without a penny of promotion--and why some multi-million-dollar advertising campaigns fail to get noticed.*

*Open your eyes to a new way of doing business--that honest marketing makes more money, because customers who trust you will talk about you.*

*Learn how to be the remarkable company that people want to share with their friends.*

## Art of War by Sun Tzu

*Sun Tzu was one of the greatest army generals who ever lived. He wrote "The Art of War" in the fifth century BC and yet his words are still resoundingly relevant to our modern lives. His writings on aspects of warfare from the laying of plans to the tactics and psychology of maneuvering an army, to the proper use of spies, resonate for us in today's world of cut-throat, ruthless business. With James Clavell's insightful foreword and notes, this classic is widely seen as a necessity on the bookshelf of military leaders and boardroom executives alike.*

The following list by Saeed Omar, Founder & CEO of SitatByoot.com, was voted as the most popular response on Quora to the question "What books should entrepreneurs read?"

## 1. Linchpin

*Teaches you to be indispensable (irreplaceable) and motivates you to dwell at the heart of your startup.*
*Say no to meaningless work, things should be looked upon from the bigger perspective —-> You should be actually working on changing the world.*
*Work the problem yourself. Imagine there were astronauts on Apollo 13 that did not know how to behave under pressure? Have they been able to solve the dire problems in real time and save everybody?*
*Lead, inspire and be responsible.*
*Linchpin is actually the word for the outer pin that holds the wheel onto the axe. A metaphor for both reliability and importance.*

## 2. Black Swan

*Black Swan stands for the overly-stated fact that all swans are White. i.e. "fair as a swan", meant that she was white as a swan. However, it took one incident of a Black Swan seeing, in newly discovered Australia, to overthrow the fact forever.*

*Past events do not predict the future.*

*There are little incidents in history that have shaped up politics and commerce. No one would have ever predicted them. So why play by the book when you can expect the unexpected?*

*Startups should know that no matter how small, their offerings can be a game changer.*

*The Gaussian way of predicting cash-flows, sales and expenses forecasts year on year, is just an obsolete way of going forward. Your new variables should be the market itself and not what you sold last year.*

*It's the Butterfly Effect: If a Butterfly flaps its wings in India, a hurricane is formed in Brazil. If you're startup launches something unique in Amman, Jordan it can sweep the world by storm.*

## 3. Tipping Point by Malcolm Gladwell

*A Tipping Point for startups is the moment of truth where your products and services pick on and become a viral buying trend.*

*Law of the few: worldwide trends do not begin big, actually you can always trace big waves down to their humble currents. i.e. PSY's Gangnam Style YouTube video.*

*You need Connectors, Mavens and Salesmen to help you connect, recommend and sell your thing respectively.*

*The Stickiness Factor: your startup service or product or even campaign should have a memorable quality. Your site's UX for that matter, should have a unique, special and addictive way of presenting your offerings.*

*Is the time and place right for your startup to pick up into mainstream? The power of Context states that you should know if you're offering can go hip in the right environment or not.*

*Harness the power of disinformation, propaganda, rumors, PR, news and underdogs to make an adoptive statement that can help raise your startup/campaign into a millionth trend.*

## 4. The Four Steps of the Epiphany

*You need to understand that 9 out of 10 startups fail in their first year. So learn the odds and play along knowingly.*

*There are 4 phases of iteration and pivoting in your startup lifespan and they are: Customer Discovery, Customer Validation, Customer Creating and then Company Building.*

*In the first phase of customer discovery, you have to tailor-make a solution for a test-market (or better even a single customer segment) that you know are out there using super-simple features. Your offering should be a Minimum Viable Product MVP.*

*The second phase is customer validation, you need to validate whatever service your customers are buying and drop those that aren't selling.*

*The third phase is when you start your customer creation by moving on from only dealing with your early-adopters. In this phase you are more confident to promote your services to a bigger market share.*

*Now you are ready to spend on building a company and spend on infrastructure, more features and employees. Everything you spend on needs to aim at scaling up and acquire more customers.*

## 5. 7 Habits of Highly effective People

*Probably the best help-book out there that helps you create a work-life balance between your emotional, physical, professional and personal lives. Why recommend this book? Because it's an essential read that should be taught at schools, me thinks. Think of it as a required 101 material before digging into other books.*

*The seven habits are: 1. Be Proactive 2. Begin with the End in mind 3. Put First Things First 4. Think Win-Win 5. Seek First to Understand, Then to Be Understood 6. Synergize 7. Sharpen the Saw*
*It teaches self-strain and how to be principle-centered.*
*One of the most important lessons in this book is time management and the diagram of 4 quadrants of Importance and Urgency. Your self-procrastinating habit will disappear after you get this straight.*

## 6. Lean Startup

*Probably the single most important book listed here - read like a programming biography of Eric Ries's trials and errors while building his startup IMVU.com.*
*Teaches you the importance of iterative project planning vs. the dangerous more linear mode; that has a beginning and an end.*
*Teaches you the importance of developing a prototype dubbed in this book as MVP.*
*When the MVP isn't acquiring the right customers then something is wrong and you have to pivot the model in order to convert them. It's all about getting customers in.*
*The concept of split-testing or A/B testing is essential when promoting new features and products.*
*Continuous development is key to success.*
*Use actionable metrics that give a realistic indication of your progress.*
*Vanity metrics by contrast will contribute to a delusional startup that has lost the plot. Metrics like number of page views, impressions, and registered users are example for Vanity metrics. While sales, conversions and referrals are metrics to measure progress on.*

## 7. Blue Ocean

*Avoid Red Ocean marketplaces where a lot of sharks swim. Because it's bloody. In another metaphor, it's a tiring rat race going after what everybody's aiming at.*

*Create the market yourself. Blue Oceans refer to markets never sought-after before because they just simply did not exist. Your entry into one is in itself a black swan. An event above predicted history. Think Steve Jobs iPod's launch event. Were there really any competition when the iPod launched? You need to add value, specifically bring in more Value Innovation to the Buyer and your Startup as a result. Buyers and beating their product satisfaction every time, take center stage here.*

*This book teaches you that big businesses are as vulnerable as you are, if they seize to provide value to the customer.*

*You can shape the industry you are in, in fact you can be the whole industry itself.*

## 8. Business Model Generation

*You do not have to go on a long Business Planning endeavor, all you need to do is outline and build 9 building blocks of your startup, using an innovative way of business planning called Business Model Generation. They are:*

*Customer Segmentation: differentiate you customers based on the variable most relevant to your startup offerings.*

*Value Proposition: ask yourself what value you bring to each?*

*Customer Relationship: what relationship you want to build with your customer?*

*Channels: what are the communication, sales and delivery channels you use with every customer segment?*

*Revenue Streams: what are your revenue streams?*

*Key Activities: define what you do as startup and team to acquire more customers?*

*Key Resources: define what are the HR, machines, programs…etc needed for you to serve your customers most efficiently?*

*Key Partners: who are your key partners that you depend on when selling your customers?*

*Cost Structure: What are your costs and how do you maintain them in relation to all your resources, partnership/supplier and activities expenses?*

# Please consider these other titles by Milford Press authors

Success and Happiness: Quotes to Motivate, Inspire and Live by - Atticus Aristotle

*"A great and easy read and one you will end up going back to time and time again if you are a quote lover such as me."*

*"Enjoyed reading all the quotes. Great book to pick up daily to motivate and inspire! Would be a good stocking stuffer"*

Quotes to Live Your Life – Atticus Aristotle

Over 1,000 inspirational quotes specifically selected for what matters the most to you: your friends, your loves, your aspirations , and the beauty which surround you.

*"This book focuses on quotes about forgiveness, charity, imagination, a life well lived, attitude, death, happiness, love, romance, friendship, inspiration, courage, art, beauty, wisdom and knowledge .... ! really enjoyed reading this book and think you will too"*

Jokes and Other Words of Wit for Everyone – Atticus Aristotle

Humorous jokes, stories, one-liners and comebacks for everyone to enjoy. This book contains jokes that can be told to anyone or anywhere without reservation, including a collection of opening lines useful for speech givers.

<u>Command Center Handbook: Proactive IT Monitoring</u> - Protecting Business Value Through Operational Excellence – Abdul A. Jaludi

Authoritative resource on command centers and using them effectively to prevent customer service disruptions and runaway technology costs through optimization, proactive and real-time monitoring.

*"This book is a clearly written 'how to' Operations playbook. It is based on IT Infrastructure Library best practices and covers all of the major processes and functions that one would require to provide high quality services and state of the art automation solutions."*

<u>The Second One: A serial killer's account of his first two kills</u> – O.M. Kiam

A short story as told by a serial killer
There's a reason why religion, faith, and a belief in an afterlife are important!
Without them man loses all moral guidance, right and wrong are left to the discretion of the individual and survival of the fittest is the law of the land.
Without religion, faith and a belief in the afterlife, there is no conscience to stop a mass murderer.

<u>Coming to Astoria: An Immigrant's Tale</u> – O.M. Kiam

Coming to Astoria takes the reader on a journey of self-discovery which is humorous, entertaining, and educational. This is a fascinating human interest story filled with poignant memories about growing up alone in a large family.

Short Story Collection – O.M. Kiam

Collection of short stories by O.M. Kiam

Hit and Run - a story of revenge
The Banking Failure - A perfect storm brings about a banking collapse
Shoe Shining - two eleven year old boys find a way to make money
The Second One: John Quinn - A serial killer's account of his first two kills
*"Five Stars - Great stories to keep you reading past bedtime."*

www.ingramcontent.com/pod-product-compliance
Lightning Source LLC
Chambersburg PA
CBHW051222170526
45166CB00005B/1998